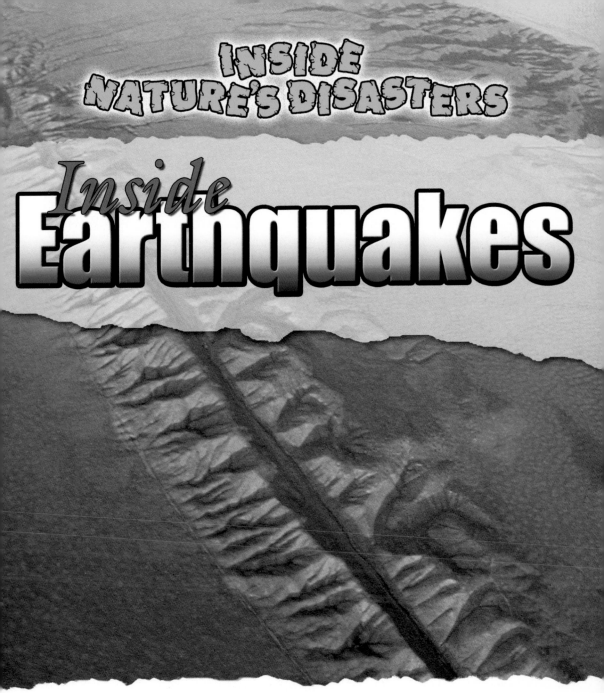

INSIDE NATURE'S DISASTERS

Inside Earthquakes

Neil Morris

GARETH STEVENS
PUBLISHING
A Member of the WRC Media Family of Companies

Please visit our web site at: www.garethstevens.com
For a free color catalog describing Gareth Stevens Publishing's
list of high-quality books and multimedia programs,
call 1-800-542-2595 or 1-800-387-3178 (Canada).
Gareth Stevens Publishing's fax: (414) 332-3567.

Library of Congress Cataloging-in-Publication Data

Morris, Neil, 1946-
   Inside earthquakes / by Neil Morris.
      p. cm. — (Inside nature's disasters)
    Includes bibliographical references and index.
    ISBN-10: 0-8368-7247-9 — ISBN-13: 978-0-8368-7247-7 (lib. bdg.)
    1. Earthquakes—Juvenile literature. I. Title. II. Series.
   QE521.3.M654   2007
   551.22—dc22   2006009691

This North American edition first published in 2007 by
Gareth Stevens Publishing
A Member of the WRC Media Family of Companies
330 West Olive Street, Suite 100
Milwaukee, WI 53212 USA

This revised and updated U.S. edition copyright © 2007 by Gareth Stevens, Inc.

Original edition copyright © 2002 by ticktock Entertainment Ltd. First published in
Great Britain in 1999 by ticktock Publishing Ltd., Unit 2, Orchard Business Centre,
North Farm Road, Tunbridge Wells, Kent, TN2 3XF.

Gareth Stevens editor: Richard Hantula
Gareth Stevens cover design: Dave Kowalski
Gareth Stevens managing editor: Mark Sachner
Gareth Stevens art direction: Tammy West

Picture Credits: t = top, b = bottom, c = center, l = left, r= right,
OFC = outside front cover, OBC = outside back cover, IFC = inside front cover
AFP/Getty Images; 18/19 (main). Ann Ronan; 8l, 13bl, 17cr, 18b, 19tr, 21t, 23c. AKG Photo;
7br, 12 (main pic), 13t, 14t, 27b, Allsport; 26b. J. Allan Cash; 21r. Stefan Chabluk; 6tr, 11c.
CORBIS; 4tl, 7tr, 15b, 16 (main) & 34, 16br, 17b, 18tl, 24-25c, 27 (main), 28bl, 28-29 (main),
29tr. Fortean; OFC (inset), 6br, 8tl, 8c, 8/9b, 9 (main pic), 10 (main pic), 10/11t, 11tr, 13cl, 15c,
17tr, 22tr, 23tr, 24t, 25r, 28tl, 30bl, 32b. Getty Images; 18/19c, 20t. The Ronald Grant Archive;
14 (main). Image Bank; 6t, 32tl. Image Select; 4b, 16b, 22b, 29br. Images; 10/11c, 33 (main). The
Kobal Collection; IFC. NASA/JPL/ESA; 30/31 (main). Pictor; 30c, 31tr. Plymouth City Museum
& Art Gallery; 15t. Science Photo Library; 22tl, 32tr. Spectrum Colour Library; 13br. Tony Stone
Images; OFC (main), 4/5c & OBC, 5 (main pic), 5tr, 11b, 20b, 20-21 (main), 21br, 23 (main),
24/25 (main), 26tl & 34.

Every effort has been made to trace the copyright holders for the photos used in this book. The
publisher apologizes, in advance, for any unintentional omissions and would be pleased to insert
the appropriate acknowledgements in any subsequent edition of this publication.

Printed in the United States of America

1 2 3 4 5 6 7 8 9 10 09 08 07 06

CONTENTS

Earthquake drill is a common practice in Japanese schools. It includes getting used to special flameproof and waterproof headgear (below).

ARISTOTLE

Aristotle (*above*; 384-322 B.C.), an ancient Greek philosopher and scientist, believed that the Earth had grown like a living thing to its present size. He also thought that our rocky planet was honeycombed with underground caves that sucked up the world's winds. When fires inside the Earth heated the winds beyond a certain point, they exploded. These explosions, Aristotle thought, caused earthquakes. A couple of thousand years passed before scientists began to discover the real cause of earthquakes.

WHAT IS AN EARTHQUAKE?

An earthquake is a shaking of the ground caused by movements beneath the Earth's surface. Strong earthquakes can collapse buildings, bridges, and other structures, causing great damage and loss of life. The Earth's surface is made up of an outer layer of rocks, called its crust. The crust is cracked into huge pieces that fit together like a giant jigsaw puzzle. These pieces, called plates, slowly move and rub against each other, squeezing and stretching the rocks and causing an enormous buildup of pressure. When the pressure becomes too great, underground rocks break and shift. This sudden release of pressure sends out shock waves that produce an earthquake and make the ground tremble at the surface. There are millions earthquakes each year worldwide, of which perhaps 50,000 or so are strong enough to be felt.

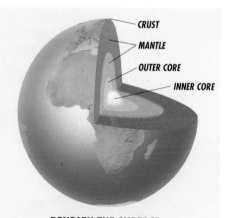

CRUST
MANTLE
OUTER CORE
INNER CORE

BENEATH THE SURFACE

Beneath the Earth's crust (*above*) is a soft mantle, made up of hot, partially molten rock. The Earth's core is made up mainly of iron and nickel, and is solid at the center. The crust can be as thick as 45 miles (70 kilometers) or more beneath the world's biggest mountain ranges. Most earthquakes begin in the crust not far below ground, but some occur up to 450 miles (700 km) beneath the surface.

ANDES MOUNTAINS

The Andes (*left*) are the longest mountain range in the world (not counting the mid-ocean ridge at the bottom of the ocean). They stretch down the whole of South America for 4,500 miles (7,200 km). They were created by the collision of the Nazca oceanic plate with the South American continental plate. In 1970 an earthquake off the Peruvian coast caused a landslide on an Andean peak; estimates of the overall death toll from the disaster reached as high as 66,000.

Curving strata are very clearly visible in this photograph (above) of a dry river valley in Namibia.

ROCK STRATA

The rocks that make up the Earth's plates are themselves made of layers, called strata. As the plates move, the strata are pushed, pulled, bent, and folded. The forces beneath the Earth are immense, but movement at the surface is very slight and folding may take thousands of years. If the strata are bent so much that they break, they form a crack called a fault.

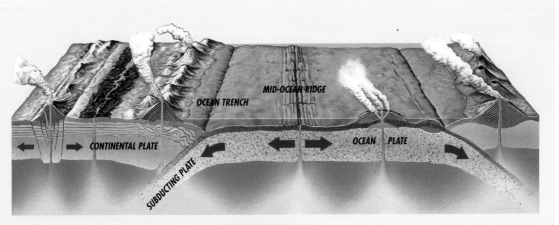

PLUNGING PLATES

Some of the world's biggest earthquakes occur in regions where two of the plates making up the Earth's rigid outer layer collide and one of them is forced beneath the other in a process called subduction (*above*). The plunging, or "subducting," plate is usually an oceanic one, covered by sea, running into a thicker continental plate, covered by land. The plunging ocean plate grinds against the upper plate, melting parts of both and creating volcanoes and earthquakes.

This satellite picture (above) shows the Ring of Fire around the Pacific Ocean. The sites of major earthquakes are marked in red.

THE WORLD'S PLATES

The plates that make up the Earth's rigid outer layer are constantly moving, at a speed of just an inch or two (a few centimeters) a year. This small movement sets off earthquakes and volcanic eruptions, as well as creating mountain ranges and deep-sea trenches. The lines on the map (*above*) show the edges of the chief plates. It is at such boundaries that most earthquakes occur.

MID-ATLANTIC RIDGE

São Miguel (*above*) is the largest of the islands that make up the Azores. This group of volcanic islands lies in the North Atlantic Ocean, about 800 miles (1,300 km) west of Portugal. The Azores are on the Mid-Atlantic Ridge, a mostly underwater range of mountains formed by molten rock as the North and South American plates move apart from the Eurasian and African plates. The islands are frequently shaken by earthquakes.

ALL OVER THE WORLD

About 150 years ago, an Irish engineer named Robert Mallet started collecting information about the exact location of earthquakes around the Mediterranean Sea. He plotted almost 7,000 earthquakes on a map and discovered a pattern, but he had no idea why this should be. We now know that about three-quarters of the world's earthquakes occur in a zone around the Pacific Ocean called the Ring of Fire. The zone gets its name from the fact that it is dotted with active volcanoes. Another earthquake belt runs across southern Europe and Asia, from the Mediterranean through the Middle East and the Himalayas to Indonesia. The two great earthquake belts meet near the island of New Guinea. Both are situated along the edges of plates.

NEW ZEALAND

The eruption of Mount Ruapehu (*above*) in 1996 was associated with earthquake activity. The Pacific and Australian Plates meet beneath the islands of New Zealand. This collision causes many earthquakes and volcanoes. New Zealand has more than 10,000 earthquakes every year, but only about 100 to 150 of them are strong enough to be felt.

CHINA

In 1556 an earthquake killed the almost unbelievable number of 830,000 people in northern China. In 1976 at least 255,000 were killed by an earthquake in Tangshan Province in the northeastern part of the country. Today, China has many cities with more than a million inhabitants. When large numbers of people live close together in or near tall buildings (*above*), the human risks from earthquakes are very high.

EUROPE

In 1997 a series of tremors in central Italy caused part of the Basilica of St. Francis in Assisi to collapse (*right*). Falling masonry killed four people, including two Franciscan friars, and many frescoes by the famous painters Giotto and Cimabue were destroyed. Through complex restoration work completed in 2006, the basilica and most of the frescoes were restored.

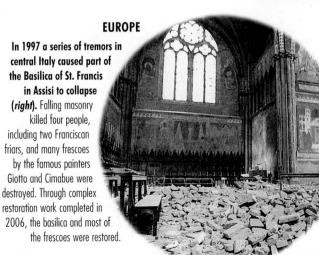

UNITED STATES

Reelfoot Lake (*above*) in Tennessee is said to have been created by earthquakes in the 19th century. Earthquakes in 1811 and 1812 centered in the vicinity of New Madrid, Missouri, were so powerful that they caused the Mississippi River to flow backward. River water poured into low-lying forests and created new lakes. Some still exist today. It is said that the quakes were so strong that they shook and rang church bells in Boston, 1,100 miles (1,700 km) away.

CRACKING FAULTS

As the plates that make up the Earth's rigid outer layer move and jostle together, they put rocks under enormous strain. The strain sometimes is so great that the rocks crack. The places where they crack are called faults, and lines tracing the cracks on the surface are known as fault lines. Large faults may go deep into underground rocks and stretch along whole continents. The world's biggest faults, like the strongest earthquakes, are found near the edges of plates. Movement along some large faults may split open the ground, and along others it may cause areas of land to rise or sink. After an earthquake, when energy has been released, the rock masses on either side of the fault are locked together in new positions. The stresses and strains that caused the original earthquake often begin again and build up until eventually they cause another quake.

A large 1992 earthquake near Landers, California, cracked and shifted this road at a horizontal fault (above). Quakes along horizontal faults can have devastating effects on buildings and other structures, and they are common in such places as California, China, and Turkey.

On the island of Iceland, a large open crack (right) marks the spot where the eastern edge of the North American Plate (at the left) meets the western edge of the Eurasian Plate (at the right). The two plates are moving apart at a rate of about an inch (2.5cm) a year, at the same time widening the Atlantic Ocean by that amount.

GREAT RIFT VALLEY

An immense system of faults runs all the way from Syria to Mozambique, cutting deep across the face of East Africa. In parts, the Great Rift Valley (*below*) is up to 60 miles (100 km) wide. It has some of Africa's most spectacular scenery, including lakes and volcanoes. Movements of the African and Somali plates, pulling apart the land, have formed much of the valley. In Kenya, this has been going on for millions of years.

NORMAL FAULT

REVERSE FAULT

HORIZONTAL FAULT

DIFFERENT FAULTS

There are different types of faults, depending on the movement of the rocks, and they fall into three main groups (*above*). A "normal" fault is caused when tension in the Earth's crust pulls two blocks of rock apart, so that one block slips down along the fault plane.
When the tension pushes two blocks of rock together, one of the blocks is forced to move up the fault plane and form a "reverse" fault.
"Horizontal" faults form when blocks of rock slide past each other sideways.

SAN ANDREAS FAULT

NORTHRIDGE, 1994

At 4:31 A.M. on January 17, 1994, the Los Angeles area was hit by a quake with its epicenter near the neighborhood called **Northridge.** The shaking, which lasted 15 to 20 seconds, knocked out several bridges and highways (*above*), killed more than 60 people, and left over 20,000 homeless. Total damage came to more than $30 billion. Northridge lies on a small fault near the San Andreas Fault.

One of the world's most famous geological features, the San Andreas Fault, runs along the Pacific coast of California. This horizontal fault is some 800 miles (1,300 km) long. It forms part of the boundary between the Pacific and North American plates. The two plates constantly slide past each other at a rate of as much as 2 inches (5 cm) a year. Many smaller fault lines crisscross the region, some connecting up with the San Andreas. This is one of the world's major earthquake zones, with thousands and thousands of tremors recorded every year.

California schoolchildren are used to earthquake drills (below left). The constant threat of earthquakes is part of their daily life and school routine.

SAN FRANCISCO, 1906

A huge earthquake hit San Francisco at 5:12 A.M. on April 18, 1906. The city shook for up to a minute as the San Andreas Fault slipped more than 20 feet (6 meters) along about 300 miles (500 km) of its length. About 28,000 buildings were destroyed by the quake and the fires it set off. At least 3,000 of the city's 400,000 people were killed, and 200,000 to 300,000 were left homeless.

The San Andreas Fault can be clearly seen from the air, like a deep scar across the landscape (left). Some scientists think that its most dangerous sections may be its two ends, at Cape Mendocino, north of San Francisco, and Imperial Valley, south of Los Angeles.

This map (left) shows how the San Andreas Fault runs along much of the California coast. The Pacific Ocean and the strip of land west of the fault lie on the Pacific Plate, which is sliding northwestward. The land east of the fault is moving very slowly toward the southeast. Los Angeles, which has a metropolitan-area population of over 16 million, is very close to the fault, and San Francisco sits practically on top of it.

NORTH AMERICAN PLATE

San Francisco

CALIFORNIA

Pacific Ocean

San Andreas Fault

PACIFIC PLATE

Los Angeles

SAN FRANCISCO, 1906

A SAN FRANCISCO JOURNALIST

The bureau at the back of the room came toward me. It was springing up and down and from side to side. It danced . . . in a zigzag course . . . it was almost funny. Now I turned on my sense of hearing. I heard the crash of falling buildings, the rumble of avalanches of bricks, the groans of tortured girders.

THE NEXT DAY

After darkness, thousands of the homeless were making their way with their blankets and scant provisions to Golden Gate Park and the beach to find shelter. Everybody is prepared to leave the city, for the belief is firm that San Francisco will be totally destroyed. Downtown everything is in ruins.

FRISCO ON FIRE

In 1906 most San Francisco buildings that withstood the shaking of the earthquake did not survive the fires (right). Many of these were caused by overturned stoves. The quake also burst water mains, leaving San Franciscans with little or no water to put out the flames. The fires raged for three days, as survivors tried to find safe areas outside the city.

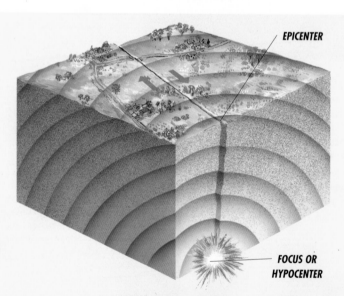

EPICENTER

FOCUS OR
HYPOCENTER

ALASKA, 1964

On March 27, 1964, the Anchorage, Alaska, region was shaken by the strongest quake in modern North American history. The shock triggered a landslide (*above*) that carried some houses built on loose rock and soil as far as 2,000 feet (600 m). The earthquake's epicenter was located about 75 miles (120 km) from Anchorage, and the focus was 14 miles (23 km) beneath the surface. The quake also created a massive ocean surge, or tsunami, that caused serious damage along the Alaskan, Canadian, and lower U.S. coasts and reached as far as Japan. The quake and its aftereffects killed more than 130 people.

FOCUS AND EPICENTER

The focus, or hypocenter, of an earthquake is deep underground, at the exact point on a fault where the rocks first crack and move. The epicenter is the point on the surface of the Earth directly above the focus. Often the pattern of seismic waves is not as neat as it appears here (*above*): waves can be bent as they pass from one type of rock to another, and body waves can be reflected back down into the ground when they reach the surface.

SEISMIC WAVES

The exact underground spot where rocks jolt and cause an earthquake is called the focus, or hypocenter. This spot may be hundreds of miles under the ground or beneath the sea. The movement of the rocks causes vibrations, called seismic waves, to travel in every direction from the focus. The seismic waves move very fast, and we feel them when they reach the surface. They are at their strongest at the quake's epicenter, the point on the Earth's surface directly above the focus. As the waves spread out from the focus, they get weaker. The general amount of damage caused by an earthquake's seismic waves depends to some extent on the kind of material doing the vibrating. Solid granite and massive layers of sandstone, for example, shake much less than the sandy soil that is often found near rivers and coasts. When rocks begin to crack along a fault, they sometimes send out a gentle tremor or series of tremors before the main earthquake. These tremors are called foreshocks, and they provide a warning for people in the region to seek a safe place.

BODY WAVES

The vibrations that travel underground from a quake's focus are called body waves. There are two kinds (below): P ("primary") waves and S ("secondary") waves. P waves are the speediest – going 13,400 miles (21,600 km) an hour in the crust, and even faster in the upper mantle. They are much faster than the speed of sound in air! P waves are pressure waves – they push and pull on rocks. S waves shake rocks up and down and from side to side in a snakelike movement.

P WAVE

S WAVE

SURFACE WAVES

At the surface there are also two kinds of seismic waves (below), named after the scientists who first described them. Rayleigh waves move up and down, and Love waves push rocks from side to side as they travel forward. Surface waves are slower than body waves, but they cause the most damage to structures on the surface, partly because they take longer to pass through.

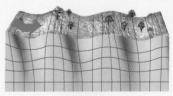

RAYLEIGH WAVE

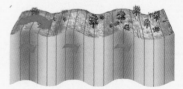

LOVE WAVE

LONG-DISTANCE DAMAGE

At 5:04 P.M. on October 17, 1989, the ground in San Francisco shook violently for 15 seconds. The earthquake killed at least 63 people, injured nearly 4,000, and caused an estimated $6 billion in property damage (*left*). Scientists discovered that the quake's epicenter was about 60 miles (100 km) south of San Francisco, near a peak called Loma Prieta in the Santa Cruz Mountains.

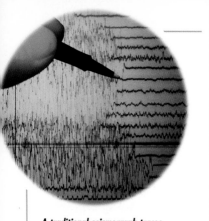

A traditional seismograph traces ground movements on paper wrapped around a rotating drum. The resulting wavy lines on a graph make up a seismogram (above). Modern computerized systems may print out the seismic data or display it on a screen. Either way, the bigger the quake, the greater the ground movement and the higher the peaks on a seismogram.

CHILE, 1960

The Richter scale doesn't work well for very large earthquakes, so seismologists very often use other scales, such as the moment magnitude scale. This is based on readings for the size of the fault's rupture, the amount of movement at the surface, and the duration of the earthquake. The resulting figure is roughly the same as the Richter figure for earthquakes up to magnitude 7. The highest moment magnitude recorded so far is 9.5, for an earthquake on the coast of Chile in 1960. The Richter magnitude of this quake was 8.3.

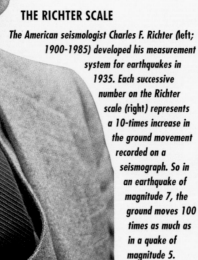

THE RICHTER SCALE

The American seismologist Charles F. Richter (left; 1900-1985) developed his measurement system for earthquakes in 1935. Each successive number on the Richter scale (right) represents a 10-times increase in the ground movement recorded on a seismograph. So in an earthquake of magnitude 7, the ground moves 100 times as much as in a quake of magnitude 5.

RICHTER MAGNITUDE	DESCRIPTION	ESTIMATED WORLD AVERAGE PER YEAR
BELOW 2	-	600,000+
2–2.9	-	300,000
3–3.9	MINOR	49,000
4–4.9	LIGHT	6,200
5–5.9	MODERATE	800
6–6.9	STRONG	120
7–7.9	MAJOR	18
8 AND ABOVE	GREAT	1

MEASUREMENT

The scientists who specialize in studying earthquakes are called seismologists. They use measuring instruments called seismographs, or seismometers, to record the pattern of seismic waves and determine the strength and duration of each earthquake. Readings are taken at several different points so that the exact location of the quake's focus and epicenter can be pinpointed. The strength of a quake's movement, based on its effects and damage, is shown as a number on a scale. An early scale measuring intensity as felt at a particular place was invented by an Italian, Guiseppe Mercalli, in 1902. The Richter scale, introduced in 1935, was the first important scale to use measurements from seismographs to assess the relative size of earthquakes. Today scientists tend to use more precise and accurate measurement systems, such as the so-called moment magnitude, in describing and comparing earthquake sizes.

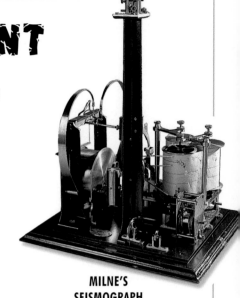

MILNE'S SEISMOGRAPH

When the British mining engineer and seismologist John Milne (1850-1913) became a professor of geology at Tokyo University, he was greeted by an earthquake on his first day in Japan. Milne set to work devising a seismograph (*above*), which recorded the motion of a pendulum, first on revolving smoked paper and later on photographic film. Milne collected data on more than 8,000 quakes in Japan alone. In 1880 he formed the Seismological Society of Japan, the first such organization anywhere in the world.

INTENSITY NEAR EPICENTER
RECORDED BUT NOT FELT
POTENTIALLY PERCEPTIBLE
FELT BY SOME
FELT BY MANY
SLIGHT DAMAGE
DAMAGING
DESTRUCTIVE
DEVASTATING

This instrument (right) was invented around A.D. 132 by a Chinese astronomer and mathematician named Zhang Heng (A.D. 78-139). Inside the pot was a pendulum, which Earth tremors would cause to swing. The swinging pendulum would knock a bronze ball from one of the dragon mouths. The ball dropped into a toad's mouth. The position of this toad showed the direction from which the tremor was coming. It is said that in A.D. 138 the seismograph allowed Zhang Heng to detect an earthquake 370 miles (600 km) away long before news of the damage arrived by messengers on horseback.

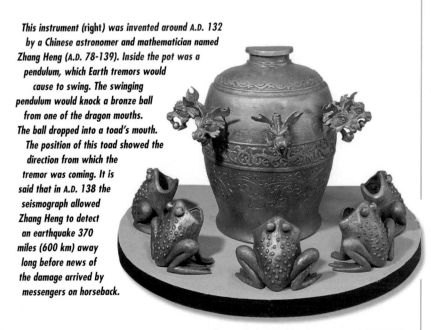

LISBON, 1755

On the morning of November 1, 1755, many of Lisbon's 275,000 citizens were in church, lighting candles for All Saints' Day. At 9:40 worshippers in the Portuguese city's central cathedral suddenly heard a terrible rumbling noise. The cathedral shook, and people ran out into the streets in time to see the ground heaving. Buildings throughout the city instantly collapsed, killing thousands of people. Many survivors ran to the harbor, but were then horrified to see huge waves — a tsunami — approaching along the Tagus River from the Atlantic Ocean. The first of these smashed over the harbor at 11:00. There was even worse to come. Within a few hours, overturned stoves and lamps started fires that were whipped up by whirling winds. A huge conflagration swept through the city, burning all the wooden structures and many of the dead bodies. This terrible earthquake, along with the resultant flooding and fires, killed more than 60,000 people in Lisbon alone.

MODERN LISBON

Lisbon was quickly rebuilt after the earthquake and today (*above*) is a popular tourist city with a metropolitan-area population of more than 2 million. The oldest part of the town has steep, narrow streets, but in the newer districts there are straight, wide streets and spacious squares. In 1966 a long suspension bridge was built across the Tagus River, and in 1998 a long cable-stayed bridge was opened.

LISBON, 1755

FROM VOLTAIRE'S CANDIDE (1759)

They felt the earth tremble beneath them. The sea boiled up in the harbor and smashed the vessels lying at anchor. Whirlwinds of flame and ashes covered the streets and squares, houses collapsed, roofs were thrown into foundations, and the foundations crumbled. . . . "This earthquake is nothing new," replied Pangloss. "The town of Lima in America felt the same shocks last year. Same causes, same effects; there is surely a vein of sulfur running underground from Lima to Lisbon."

CITY IN RUINS

About three-quarters of all Lisbon's buildings were destroyed (*above*). Records show that all of the city's 40 parish churches were damaged, and half were completely ruined. Fires burned throughout the city for days. Priceless paintings by masters such as Titian, Rubens, and Correggio were burned to ashes. Most survivors left Lisbon, and many set up camp in the hills.

16

LISABONA

This engraving (left) shows the earthquake's catastrophic effects on Lisbon. Waves are overwhelming ships in the harbor. Some buildings have been swept out to sea, and fires are raging. It is thought that one of the huge sea waves was as high as 40 feet (12 m). Seismologists think the magnitude of the quake may have been as great as 8.7. They believe the epicenter was on the bed of the Atlantic Ocean, perhaps near the edge of the Eurasian and African plates. It is said that as a result of the quake and tsunami, church bells began to peal thousands of miles away, waves appeared on the surface of Loch Ness in Scotland, and canal boats in Amsterdam were ripped from their moorings.

KANT

The German philosopher Immanuel Kant (*above;* 1724-1804) reported that eight days before the earthquake, the ground near Cadiz, a Spanish port down the coast from Lisbon, was covered with worms that had suddenly crawled out of the soil. This was not the first report of strange behavior by animals before earthquakes and other disasters, and it was of great interest to scientists.

Engraved for the General Magazine of Arts & Sciences, Printed for W.ᵐ Owen at Temple Bar.

A General View of the CITY of LISBON the Capital of the Kingdom of Portugal before the late dreadful Earthquake on Nov.ᵗʰ1ˢᵗ 1755.

This painting (above) shows how the port of Lisbon looked before the great earthquake. It was made the capital of Portugal in 1256 and quickly became one of Europe's leading cities. It was the chief port serving the vast Portuguese Empire.

TSUNAMIS

Seaquakes – earthquakes that occur beneath the ocean floor – can create huge waves that sweep across the ocean. These are called tsunamis, from the Japanese for "harbor waves," because they are very destructive when they reach harbors, or any coastline. Tsunamis are sometimes called tidal waves, but that name is misleading because they have nothing to do with tides. Some are due to underwater volcanic eruptions and landslides, but many are caused by quakes that shake the ocean floor and then the water above. That was the case with the devastating Indian Ocean tsunami of December 2004, which killed approximately 200,000 people. In the open ocean, a tsunami may move as fast as 600 miles (1,000 km) an hour. The speeding wave may be just 12 inches (30 cm) high over deep water. But as it reaches shallower water near the coast, it slows down and at the same time builds up to its greatest height, which may exceed 100 feet (30 m).

EASTER ISLAND

The great Chilean earthquake of 1960 sent tsunami waves across the Pacific Ocean. On their way they hit the small volcanic Easter Island, which is about 2,300 miles (3,700 km) from the Chilean coast. The tsunami knocked over some of the mysterious ancient stone statues for which the island is famous (*above*).

INDONESIA, 2004

The village of Sirombu (above) on the Indonesian island of Nias lay in ruins at the end of 2004 after it was hit by a powerful earthquake and tsunami.

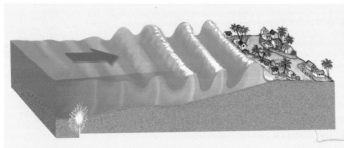

HOW IT FORMS

If an earthquake shakes the seabed, and thus the water lying above, a tsunami may result, building up as it nears the shore (left). A Tsunami Warning Center for the Pacific, where most damaging tsunamis occur, is based in Hawaii. Advance warnings give people time to evacuate coastal areas. Unfortunately, such a warning system did not exist for the Indian Ocean in December 2004.

THAILAND, 2004

The devastating Indian Ocean tsunami of December 2004 hits a beach in Thailand. In this dramatic photo (above), a woman turns toward the huge wave to warn others to head for shore. Although they were unable to escape the wave, everyone shown here survived.

NICARAGUA, 1992

On the evening of September 1, 1992, two men were sitting in their boat in the harbor of the Nicaraguan port of San Juan del Sur. Darkness fell. Suddenly they heard a thump as their boat struck the harbor floor – the water at that spot was normally more than 20 feet (6 m) deep. The two men struggled to keep their boat from capsizing and then looked toward the port. They could see the lights of the town through the crest of the wave that had just passed beneath their boat. Then the lights went out. The port had been hit by a tsunami.

NICARAGUA, 1992

On September 1, 1992, a seaquake of magnitude 7 shook the Pacific Ocean floor, 60 miles (100 km) off the Nicaraguan coast in Central America. Many Nicaraguans did not even feel the ground tremble, but soon a stretch of coastline 200 miles (320 km) long was hit by tsunamis as high as 30 feet (10 m). The waves killed about 170 people and left more than 13,000 homeless (*above*).

PAKISTAN

An earthquake in October 2005 in the Pakistan-held region of Kashmir killed close to 100,000 people and left millions homeless. Two months later, with winter beginning, many still lived in tents (*right*).

INDIA, 1993
BURIED FOR FIVE DAYS

Early on the morning of September 30, 1993, a large earthquake hit the Indian state of Maharashtra, killing approximately 10,000 people. It completely destroyed 17 villages and badly damaged a further 119. In the village of Magrul, an 18-month-old baby named Priya was trapped beneath the rubble. Five days later she still had not been found, and her mother, who was in the hospital with severe injuries, had almost given up hope. Then, as rescuers continued digging, baby Priya was found, alive and well. The only worry for the rescuers was that she would not accept a drink from anybody. They sent for her grandmother. When the grandmother offered water, Priya drank. She just would not accept anything from strangers. When she got a little older, she said she wanted to become a doctor when she grew up.

KAZAKHSTAN

Almaty, the largest city in Kazakhstan in central Asia, has a population of more than a million. The city is in a valley in the foothills of the Tian Shan mountain range (*left*), and the region is very prone to landslides. Almaty itself was virtually destroyed by earthquakes in 1887 and 1911, and in 1921 a mudflow caused great damage. In an effort to keep this from happening again, engineers used an explosion to deliberately set off a landslide in 1966. The landslide blocked up a gorge, and when another natural mudflow occurred in 1973, its effects on the area's residents were greatly reduced.

LOOKING FOR SURVIVORS

In 1970 an earthquake-triggered landslide and avalanche on Mount Huascaran in Peru buried the town of Yungay, killing more than 17,000 people. Landslides are so common in the Andes Mountains that the International Union of Geological Sciences started a program using radar satellites to track them so that scientists could learn more about landslides and mudflows and try to predict them in the future.

These people (right) are searching for survivors following a landslide in Peru in 1963, seven years before the terrible Mount Huascarn disaster.

LANDSLIDES AND MUDFLOWS

Earthquakes often set off landslides, especially on steep mountains and coastal cliffs, that engulf everything in their paths. Where there is sandy soil or clay, a slight vibration can bring down a whole slope. In 1920 an earthquake in northern China started a landslide of loose soil that killed 200,000 people. Large rockfalls can be catastrophic, too. An earthquake off the coast of Peru in 1970 started a landslide and avalanche of glacier ice on Mount Huascaran, the highest peak in the Peruvian Andes; two towns were buried. Estimates of the total death toll in the quake and its aftermath ran as high as 66,000. Heavy rain can also cause rocks and soil loosened by earthquakes to flow downhill in a "mudflow."

RESCUE SERVICES

In the Andes Mountains and elsewhere one of the great problems facing rescue services is how to reach people who need help quickly. Landslides and mudflows wreck roads and railway lines. Helicopters (*above*) are the most effective means of rescue. Even if they cannot land, they can hoist people up from the ground, or lower or drop medical and food supplies.

HUMAN-MADE QUAKES

Earthquakes are caused by natural forces. But it is possible for humans to trigger quakes, or at least make them more likely, by affecting the outer layer of the Earth. Underground nuclear explosions, which used to be frequently carried out in desert regions, release tremendous energy and act like earthquakes. Putting water into the ground can also cause tremors. This was discovered when wastewater from a chemical weapons factory was pumped into a "deep-injection well" at the Rocky Mountain Arsenal near Denver, Colorado. It was stopped when scientists realized that earth tremors increased as more water was pumped in. Many dam projects have also been blamed for earthquakes — the water in reservoirs weighs down on the ground below and seeps into cracks and faults.

CONTROLLING THE NILE

Before the Aswan High Dam was built in Egypt to hold back the waters of the Nile River, two temples constructed by Ramses II at Abu Simbel over 3,000 years ago were cut into blocks and moved to higher ground (*above*) to save them from flooding. The Aswan Dam was opened in 1971, creating Lake Nasser, a reservoir more than 300 miles (500 km) long. There were no records of any large quakes in the area, but in 1981 it was hit by a magnitude-5.3 quake. The epicenter was about 40 miles (60 km) upstream from the dam, along a fault near the lake.

HOOVER DAM

The Hoover Dam (*left*) holds back the waters of the Colorado River at the end of the Grand Canyon, on the Arizona–Nevada border. When the dam was completed in 1936, it created an enormous reservoir called Lake Mead. As the reservoir filled up, tremors were felt in the region. When it was almost full, a magnitude-5 earthquake rattled the city of Las Vegas, 30 miles (50 km) away. Fortunately, no damage was done to the dam, and the tremors died away. Today the Hoover Dam supplies water and hydroelectric power over a wide area.

In 1997, villagers near a new reservoir in Lesotho, in southern Africa, fled when a crack 1 mile (1.5 km) long and up to 3 inches (7 cm) wide opened up in their village. People in the Lesotho highlands felt many small tremors after the Katse Reservoir (*right*) began to fill in 1995.

LAKE KARIBA

The Kariba Dam, on the Zambezi River at the Zambia/Zimbabwe border in southern Africa, made a lake eight times bigger than the lake created by the Hoover Dam. As Lake Kariba was filling up between 1958 and 1961, the region was shaken by thousands of tremors. The biggest was magnitude 5.8. The tremors became fewer once the reservoir was full.

Parts of the region around Lake Kariba (above) have been made into a nature reserve.

WATER PRESSURE

We now know that underground water can cause pressure to build up and rocks to slip (*right*). In an experiment carried out at Rangely, Colorado, scientists pumped water at high pressure into deep oil wells. They measured the amount of water absorbed by the underground rocks and used seismographs to check for tremors. They found that the higher the water pressure, the more small tremors were recorded. It appeared that the water lubricated faults in the rocks, causing them to slip and shake the ground.

MEXICO CITY, 1985

The western coast of Mexico forms part of the Ring of Fire that surrounds the Pacific Ocean. Here the Cocos Plate beneath the ocean slides slowly under the lighter North American Plate, forming a deep underwater trench. At 7:18 A.M. on September 19, 1985, rocks slipped along a 120-mile (200-km) fault in this region, moving a distance of 7 feet (2 m) in two separate jerks, 27 seconds apart. The focus of the earthquake was 12 miles (20 km) below the surface, near the coast of the Mexican state of Michoacan. The quake, of magnitude 8.1, released a thousand times more energy than the atomic bomb dropped on Hiroshima, Japan, in World War II. One minute later, the seismic waves reached Mexico City, 240 miles (380 km) away, rolling in at 15,000 miles (24,000 km) per hour. Within five minutes, more than 400 buildings in the city collapsed, and a further 3,000 were badly damaged. Official figures listed 9,500 people dead, but some sources put the total much higher.

AZTEC CAPITAL

According to legend, the Aztecs were told to settle where they found a special sign — an eagle on a cactus grasping a snake (*above*). Around 1325 they found it, on a marshy island in Lake Texcoco, and built their capital, Tenochtitlan, there. The Aztec capital was destroyed by Spanish conquerors in 1521, and Mexico City was built in its place. When the earthquake struck in 1985, the vibrations intensified in the old lake bed, rattling the buildings in the city above.

MONITORING THE QUAKE

At the U.S. National Earthquake Information Center in Golden, Colorado, alarms were set off at 7:23 A.M., four minutes after Mexico City shook. Surface waves were monitored as they arrived at Golden, about 1,500 miles (2,500 km) from the epicenter, another five minutes later. The Information Center (*right*) issues reports on quakes around the world, and has located hundreds of thousands of quakes since settling in Golden in 1974.

Tenochtitlan, the Aztec capital, was a city of islands linked by canals. The waterways and gardens of Xochimilco (right), to the south of present-day Mexico City, are all that is left of the canals.

MEXICO CITY

A family who lived on the ground floor of a 14-floor apartment building believe they were saved by their pet parrot. The building collapsed on top of them, and the parrot started screaming. Rescuers heard the screams and managed to reach the buried family eight hours later.

SEARCHING THE WRECKAGE

Rescue workers were able to pull many survivors from the wreckage of collapsed apartment buildings. More than 30,000 people were injured, and at least 100,000 were left homeless. Survivors may sometimes be trapped for days in collapsed buildings. Rescuers have the difficult task of locating survivors and then moving rubble safely. Specially trained dogs (*right*) and infrared or heat-sensitive equipment are used to help rescuers find people. In poorer regions of the world, where such equipment is not available, the rescue services have a much more difficult job.

CLEANING UP

In 1985, Mexico City had a total population of about 18 million. Most of its people were affected in some way by the quake (above). Many of those who lost their homes were housed in tents until new accommodation could be found. At first they simply had to look after themselves. Disease can easily spread after any natural disaster if there is a lack of clean water and healthy food. Some of the collapsed buildings were hospitals, and rescuers searching for survivors found a total of 58 newborn babies beneath the ruins. Some had been buried for up to seven days. It is thought they survived because their bodies behaved as though they were still in the womb.

HONSHU, JAPAN

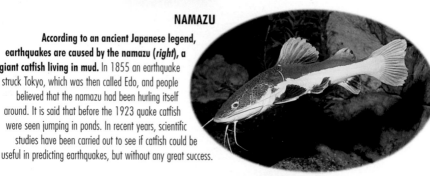

TOKYO, 1923

Survivors of the 1923 quake searched among the rubble for their lost possessions (*above*). Huge fires had broken out in Tokyo, as overturned stoves set wooden houses ablaze. The fires caused most of the casualties. As a result of the quake, some areas around the city were lifted up by 7 feet (2 m), and the floor of Tokyo Bay moved 10 feet (3 m) northward. The nearby city of Yokohama was also badly hit. A *London Times* correspondent reported that Yokohama had been "wiped off the map."

Japan is situated where four of the Earth's plates meet – the Eurasian and North American Plates to the north, and the Philippine and Pacific Plates to the south. So it is not surprising that the islands have many volcanoes and suffer thousands of earthquakes every year. Most of the quakes are quite mild, but on September 1, 1923, a quake of magnitude 7.9 shook a huge area of Honshu, Japan's largest island, including Japan's capital city, Tokyo. Over half a million houses were reduced to rubble, and 143,000 people died, 100,000 in Tokyo alone. Then, in 1995, the very south of the island, about 275 miles (440 km) from Tokyo, was hit. The industrial port of Kobe suffered the worst damage, as buildings collapsed and ruptured gas mains burst into flames all over the city. Many of Kobe's newer buildings survived, however, because they had been built with earthquakes in mind.

KOBE, 1995

The Kobe quake struck at 5:47 A.M. on January 17, 1995, and measured 6.9 in magnitude. The city of Kobe shook for 20 seconds, and the concrete pillars holding up a section of the Hanshin Expressway linking Kobe with Osaka collapsed. Parts of the elevated expressway toppled and crashed (*left*). In all, more than 5,000 people were killed by the earthquake.

NAMAZU

According to an ancient Japanese legend, earthquakes are caused by the namazu (*right*), a giant catfish living in mud. In 1855 an earthquake struck Tokyo, which was then called Edo, and people believed that the namazu had been hurling itself around. It is said that before the 1923 quake catfish were seen jumping in ponds. In recent years, scientific studies have been carried out to see if catfish could be useful in predicting earthquakes, but without any great success.

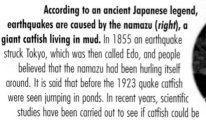

LIVING WITH QUAKES

Japanese children are used to performing earthquake drills. This includes familiarizing themselves with special flameproof and waterproof headgear (*above*). In Tokyo, September 1 is known as Disaster Prevention Day. On the anniversary of the terrible Tokyo quake, remembrance services are held for victims.

EVACUEES

The Kobe earthquake destroyed 100,000 houses, and another 88,000 were badly damaged. More than 300,000 people were evacuated from their homes, and many lived in refugee camps for weeks (*above*); 70,000 people were still living in shelters two months after the quake. During this period there were thousands of small aftershocks, which made many believe that another major earthquake was on its way. Fortunately, that didn't happen.

The Kobe quake broke the city's water mains. About a million homes were without water for 10 days, so people had to stand in line for small supplies. Gas and electricity were also shut off, and 2 million homes were left without power.

TOKYO & KOBE

It was discovered that a 90-year-old woman rescued from her home after the Kobe earthquake had also been a victim of the Tokyo quake 72 years earlier. In 1923 she was working in an office in Yokohama, and hid under a desk to avoid being crushed when the building collapsed. She moved some years later when her husband was transferred by his company from Yokohama to Kobe.

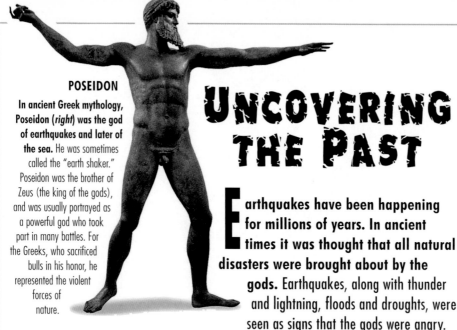

POSEIDON

In ancient Greek mythology, Poseidon (*right*) was the god of earthquakes and later of the sea. He was sometimes called the "earth shaker." Poseidon was the brother of Zeus (the king of the gods), and was usually portrayed as a powerful god who took part in many battles. For the Greeks, who sacrificed bulls in his honor, he represented the violent forces of nature.

UNCOVERING THE PAST

Earthquakes have been happening for millions of years. In ancient times it was thought that all natural disasters were **brought about by the gods.** Earthquakes, along with thunder and lightning, floods and droughts, were seen as signs that the gods were angry.

Three of the Seven Wonders of the Ancient World — the Mausoleum, the Colossus of Rhodes, and the lighthouse known as the Pharos of Alexandria — were shaken to the ground by quakes. The first great palace built by the Minoans at Knossos, in Crete, had already suffered this fate around 1700 B.C. The citizens of the Roman cities of Pompeii and Herculaneum felt very strong tremors and suffered damage in A.D. 63, 16 years before Mount Vesuvius erupted and destroyed both. But at that time little or nothing was known about the links between earthquakes and volcanoes.

THE FIRST MAUSOLEUM

Mausolus was ruler of Caria, part of the Persian Empire. He planned a huge tomb, the Mausoleum, for himself and his Queen, Artemisia, and it was completed shortly after his death in 353 B.C. In the 13th century A.D., the Mausoleum was knocked down by an earthquake. Hundreds of years later statues and sculptures, such as these (*right*), which archaeologists believe show the king and queen, were excavated at the site in modern-day Turkey.

The Pharos lighthouse (right) was built in the third century B.C. to guide ships safely into the harbor of Alexandria, in Egypt. It was probably the world's first lighthouse. At the top was a fire, and sheets of bronze reflected its light out to sea. An earthquake destroyed the Pharos in the 14th century A.D., and some years later Muslims used the ruins to build a military fort.

KOURION, CYPRUS

In A.D. 365 a great earthquake struck the eastern Mediterranean region. Scientists believe that its epicenter was on the seafloor, about 30 miles (50 km) off the coast of Cyprus. The quake killed thousands on that island, and at the coastal town of Kourion archaeologists have discovered skeletons, pots, vases, and many other artifacts, such as this mosaic (*left*), beneath the ruins.

TEMPLE OF ZEUS

The ancient Greeks worshipped Zeus, king of the gods, at Olympia. An enormous statue of Zeus, made of ivory, gold, and precious stones, stood in a temple there and became one of the Wonders of the World. Some believe it was shipped to Constantinople in the fifth century A.D. In any case, in the sixth century the Olympia region was shaken by earthquakes. The temple and Olympia's famous stadium were destroyed by landslides and floods; they were not excavated until recent times. Just a few columns (*above*) remain today.

Today, a bronze deer (right) stands on a pillar at each side of the entry to Mandraki Harbor, where the Colossus may have stood.

A FALLEN STATUE

Mandraki Harbor, on the Greek island of Rhodes, was believed to be protected by a giant bronze statue of Helios, the sun god. The statue, called the Colossus, is said to have had one foot on each side of the harbor entrance (*right*), but around 226 B.C. it was toppled by an earthquake and snapped off at the knees. The people of Rhodes were told by an oracle not to rebuild the statue, so they left it lying where it fell.

SATELLITE VIEWS

Space satellites use various technologies to observe the Earth's surface. Iran's Shahdad region (*top*) is earthquake prone. Radar can be used to construct an image (*bottom*) revealing hidden details of faults and movements in the region.

HAICHENG

Early in 1975, seismologists noticed that water levels in wells around the city of Haicheng, in northeast China (*right*), were changing. Then small tremors started. Around a million people were evacuated from their homes in the region on the morning of February 4, and that evening a magnitude 7.3 earthquake struck. Thousands of buildings collapsed, and more than 2,000 people were killed. Without the warning, probably many thousands more would have died.

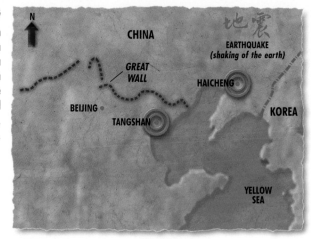

N

CHINA

地震
EARTHQUAKE
(*shaking of the earth*)

GREAT
WALL

HAICHENG

BEIJING

KOREA

TANGSHAN

YELLOW
SEA

CHECKING GROUNDWATER

The amounts of minerals and gases that are present in groundwater can change before an earthquake, as rocks move and the water is squeezed from one crack to another. For this reason, water levels are checked regularly (above).

TANGSHAN

Less than 18 months after the Haicheng quake, a much greater disaster struck Tangshan Province. This time there was no forecast and no warning. The epicenter of a magnitude 7.5 quake was right by the city of Tangshan (*above*), just 250 miles (400 km) from Haicheng. The results were catastrophic — made worse by a powerful aftershock 15 hours after the main quake. The official death toll for the two quakes was 255,000, but some researchers believe more than half a million people died.

PREDICTING EARTHQUAKES

Seismologists are constantly looking for new methods that will help them forecast when and where major earthquakes will occur. Some scientists believe that strong earthquakes are less likely to happen in areas where weak quakes are common because the small tremors relieve the stress that otherwise would lead to a major jolt. In high-risk areas in the United States and Japan, experiments are being conducted to detect the tiniest movements along fault lines. Scientists hope that this will help them predict a possible larger movement in the future, so that people can be evacuated from danger zones. Researchers have also found that changes in the level and content of underground water can reveal a lot about the movement and possible cracking of rocks.

CREEPMETERS

Creepmeters, which measure the creep, or movement, of a fault, can be used to detect minute changes. This technician (*above*) is checking a creepmeter at Parkfield, California. Scientists believe that the more data they can acquire about small ground movements over many years, the easier it will become to recognize changes in the normal pattern — changes that might show a big quake is on its way.

MONITORING PARKFIELD

Parkfield lies on California's San Andreas Fault, almost exactly halfway between San Francisco and Los Angeles. It is the most intensely monitored section of any earthquake zone in the world. The arrows (*below*) show the directions in which movement along the fault is slowly occurring.

❶ An underground seismometer measures the smallest tremor.

❷ A magnetometer measures changes in the Earth's magnetic field, which tell scientists about stress on underground rocks.

❸ A seismometer near the surface records larger tremors.

❹ A vibrating instrument creates shock waves to probe the earthquake zone.

❺ A creepmeter measures ground movement at the surface very precisely.

❻ A strainmeter measures any underground deformation of rock produced by strain, and transmits this to a satellite.

❼ A sensor constantly checks groundwater level; the results are also sent to the satellite.

❽ A space satellite receives data from Parkfield and beams the information to a main geological survey station.

❾ Lasers measure any ground movement across the fault by bouncing beams off reflectors ❿.

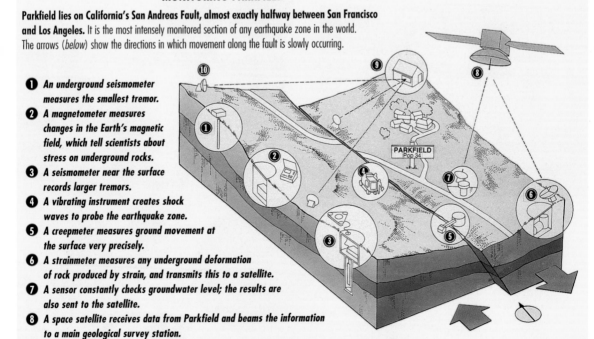

LOOKING TO THE FUTURE

SHOCK ABSORBERS

Rubber and steel pads, called isolators, can be put under new or existing buildings to make them more earthquake-resistant — just as was done with this ancient Roman statue (*above*) in a California museum. The isolators act as shock absorbers, and the space around them lets the building shake without collapsing. Tall buildings must be able to sway without cracking, just as they do in high winds. To make them safer, walls are made of reinforced concrete and are strengthened with steel beams.

Scientists have tried to find ways of reducing the strength of earthquakes — for example, by pumping water into the ground to lubricate faults and allow rocks to slide past each other with less shock and more warning. So far these experiments have not been very successful, and we will probably never be able to stop earthquakes. However, we can try to learn much more about them so that we can issue precautions and warnings that could help save lives and keep cities and towns from being destroyed. Buildings can be constructed with earthquakes in mind, and modern technology can be used to forecast where and when disasters are likely to happen.

LEARNING MORE

The more we learn about earthquakes, the better we will be able to survive them. Researchers worldwide share information about past quakes and possible future ones. They collect data using equipment such as these banks of seismographs and other devices (*above*) at the U.S. Geological Survey's laboratories in Menlo Park, California. They also use computer programs that can project what might happen in a given area if a quake were to strike.

LEADERS IN EARTHQUAKE RESEARCH

Japan ranks among the world leaders in seismological research. The Building Research Institute in Tsukuba has one of the largest earthquake study facilites in the world (*above*). There, architects and engineers test models of new buildings with vibrating machines that produce the same effect as an earthquake and can be regulated by magnitude. The models are tested until destruction occurs in order to find out how much vibration they can withstand. Technicians map every crack after the simulated tremors.

SURVIVAL KIT

In earthquake zones many homes and offices have survival kits containing equipment and supplies (left, right, below) that can help people stay alive if they are trapped for a long time.

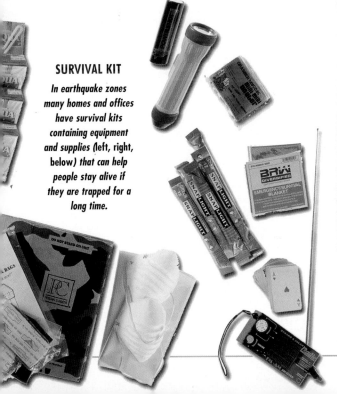

The pyramid-shaped Transamerica Building (above) in San Francisco was designed to withstand earthquakes. The 48-floor skyscraper is the city's tallest building, with a total height (including spire) of 853 feet (260 m).

DID YOU KNOW?

Worldwide, more than 1.5 million people died in earthquakes in the 20th century.

The Great Alaskan Earthquake of 1964 — with a magnitude of 9.2 the largest quake ever recorded in North America — rumbled on for at least four minutes.

The Indian Ocean tsunami that killed some 200,000 people at the end of 2004 was set off by a magnitude 9.0 earthquake off the west coast of northern Sumatra, Indonesia. Just three months later, northern Sumatra was shaken by another powerful quake, of magnitude 8.7, which killed more than 1,000 people.

Light flashes might provide a warning of some earthquakes. Survivors said they saw flashes of white, orange, or blue light shortly before the Kobe earthquake struck in 1995. Various possible explanations have been suggested for this, including "fractoluminescence" — light produced when a crystalline material such as quartz is fractured.

Prisoners have escaped from jail during many of the world's major earthquakes. One escapee was Captain "Red Legs" Greaves, a famous pirate who reputedly never robbed the poor or mistreated his own prisoners. Tried and sentenced to be hanged for piracy, he escaped in 1680 when an earthquake destroyed the prison on the Caribbean island of Nevis where he was held. He later won a pardon.

The American architect and engineer Julia Morgan (1872–1957) built a bell-tower of reinforced concrete in San Francisco in 1904. There were very few woman architects in those days, and the use of reinforced concrete was considered very unusual. But when the structure withstood the terrible 1906 earthquake, Morgan's reputation was made.

Earthquakes have helped us learn about our ancestors. A case in point is Olduvai Gorge, part of the Great Rift Valley. This archaeological site, located in the Serengeti Plains in northern Tanzania, has provided scientists with unique evidence for early human evolution from millions of years ago. A prehistoric earthquake cut through the plains and formed the jagged rift of the gorge, exposing the shores of a dried-up lake to view. Many remains of early humanlike creatures have been found in the region.

During the first Moon landing in 1969, astronauts Neil Armstrong and Edwin "Buzz" Aldrin set up scientific instruments on the moon, including a seismometer. Before long the first evidence of a "moonquake" had been sent back to Earth.

Florida and North Dakota are the U.S. states with the fewest earthquakes, and Alaska and California the states with the most. In fact, Alaska has more quakes every year than all the other states put together.

Landslides cause an average of $1 billion to $2 billion in damage and over 25 deaths in the United States every year.

GLOSSARY

aftershock - a small earthquake that follows a large quake and occurs in the same general area

body waves - seismic, or earthquake, waves that travel underground, within the Earth; two types are P ("primary" or "pressure") waves and S ("secondary") waves

core - the ball-shaped central part of the Earth, composed mostly of iron and nickle and lying below the mantle

crust - the thin, solid outer layer of the Earth; it is thinner under the oceans than the continents, where its thickness averages about 25 miles (40 km) and can be as much as 45 miles (70 km) or more in mountainous areas

epicenter - the point on the Earth's surface right above the focus, or hypocenter, of an earthquake

fault - in a large mass of rock, a crack or break at which movement has occurred

focus - or hypocenter, the exact place within the Earth where rock movement occurs that causes an earthquake

foreshock - a small earthquake that precedes a large quake and occurs in the same general area

mantle - the layer within the Earth that lies between the crust and the mantle; it is about 1,800 miles (2,900 km) thick

mid-ocean ridge - a raised section of the ocean floor running along a rift where two oceanic plates are moving apart; the

plate - or tectonic plate, one of several rigid pieces that make up the Earth's outer layer; movements of the plates play a role in many earthquakes and the formation of many volcanoes

Richter scale - a system of numbers measuring the relative size of earthquakes based on seismograph readings; scientists these days tend to use other scales that are more precise and accurate, such as the moment magnitude scale

rift - a crack where pieces of the Earth's surface, such as two plates, are moving apart

San Andreas Fault - a fault that runs for about 800 miles (1,300 km) in California; it lies on the boundary between the Pacific and North American plates

seismograph - a device that detects and records seismic, or earthquake, waves

strata - layers of rock

subduction - the process that occurs when two tectonic plates collide and the edge of one plate descends below the other and enters the mantle

surface waves - seismic, or earthquake, waves that travel along Earth's surface, such as Rayleigh waves and Love waves

tremor - a small earthquake, especially one preceding or following a major quake

tsunami - a powerful, rapidly moving ocean wave produced by an underwater earthquake, volcano eruption, or landslide; tsunamis can be very destructive

INDEX